WHEN ANGELS STEP IN

When Angels Step In

KAREN KAZIMER SHOCKLEY

Contents

Introduction

We live in a world filled with mysteries. Some are explained by science, logic, or reason. But others—well, they demand something more. They hint at the divine, the miraculous, the unseen forces that walk alongside us: Angels, to be exact. We've all heard of them. Angels, those ethereal beings who save us in ways we can't explain, perhaps earning their wings when a bell rings.

To many, angels seem distant, like figures from ancient stories or lofty ideals reserved for the exceptionally faithful. They appear as something apart from daily life, untouched by the mess and chaos of our world.

But for me, they *are* my daily life. Countless times, I've faced moments that defy explanation. Coincidences are too perfect to be random. Near misses that left me awestruck. Comfort that came when I needed it most, though no one else was in the room. These experiences have taught me to see beyond the visible, to believe in the beings we often can't see clearly but know in our hearts are there.

I prefer to live in a world where angels guide and intercede. Where the impossible becomes possible, and the inexplicable becomes proof of divine love.

This book isn't about convincing you to believe. It's not about proving anything to skeptics or arguing theology. It's simply about sharing my truth—the experiences that have shaped my life and my faith. The moments where I know, without a doubt, that angels have been with me and those I know.

So, let me take you into my world. A world where the ordinary meets the extraordinary, where heaven seems just a breath away, and where the kindness of unseen hands can change everything.

These are my stories. My encounters. My belief in beings who may be invisible but are never absent.

If there was ever a place you'd want your guardian angel right by your side, the beach would certainly be it.

Now, for those unfamiliar with guardian angels, let me explain: these aren't the kind of angels you see on greeting cards or dangling from keychains. No, these are the unseen protectors, assigned to each of us by God, watching over our steps, nudging us away from danger with quiet urgency. They're the ones who whisper "buckle your seatbelt" right before an unexpected slam on the brakes, or who guide your car just a few

Chapter 1

Chapter One - Julia's Angel at the Beach

Angel Hovering Over a Shoreline

The beach has always been a special place for our family—a sanctuary of sunshine, salty breezes, and the simple joy of being together. But it's also been the backdrop for more than one quiet prayer whispered into the sea air, especially when something precious has gone missing. Of all those moments, one stands out in my memory with a clarity that still makes me pause and smile.

It was a hot summer day on the Outer Banks of North Carolina, the kind of day when the sun seems determined to toast every shoulder it touches and the ocean roars with an open invitation to jump in. If you've ever been to the Outer Banks, you know how it is. The beaches stretch on forever, but somehow, every inch of sand is covered—blanket to blanket—with families, couples, and solo sun-seekers trying to soak in the magic of summer.

That morning, we claimed a modest patch of beach real estate between two colorful umbrellas and laid out our towels and chairs. Coolers were unpacked, flip-flops tossed aside, and the scent of sunscreen filled the air as we settled in for a day of surf and sun.

Julia, my daughter, was about ten at the time—a sweet, thoughtful girl with curly blonde hair and a quiet sense of responsibility well beyond her years. Before dashing into the waves with her boogie board under one arm, she paused beside me.

"Mom," she said, tugging on my arm, "I'm going to take off my jewelry. I don't want to lose it in the water."

Smart girl. I watched as she carefully removed her little silver dolphin necklace, a friendship ring she'd gotten for her birthday, and a tiny charm bracelet she'd picked out herself the week before. Each piece meant something to her—not expensive, but special.

"I'll put it right here," she said, and knelt at the edge of our blanket.

She scooped a shallow hole into the sand and tucked her treasures inside, then covered them back up with a practiced hand, patting it down and brushing a corner of the blanket just over the spot. "There," she said with a nod of satisfaction. "Safe and sound."

I smiled. "Good thinking, sweetheart. Let's just remember to grab it before we go."

And with that, she sprinted toward the water, her laughter joining the rhythm of the waves.

The day passed in a blur of sunscreen reapplications, sandy sandwiches, and collecting seashells in plastic buckets. We built lopsided castles, played frisbee near the shoreline, and laughed until our stomachs hurt. When the shadows grew longer and the sun softened into a golden hue, we packed up and headed into town for dinner—sandy, sun-kissed, and content.

It wasn't until we were seated at a casual seafood spot—cold drinks in hand, the smell of fried shrimp in the air—that I heard the dreaded two syllables.

"Uh-oh."

My fork paused halfway to my mouth. I turned and saw Julia, wide-eyed, pale, and frozen mid-thought. Her lips parted again, and this time her voice was quieter, hesitant.

"Mom... I left my jewelry at the beach."

For a second, we just stared at each other. I could see the realization washing over her, followed by the rising tide of panic.

"Oh no," she whispered, her voice trembling. "It's buried in the sand. We didn't go back for it. I forgot. I'm so sorry—what should I do?"

I reached over and took her hand, squeezing it gently. "First, take a deep breath," I said, trying to sound calm even though my mind was already calculating how unlikely it was we'd ever find that jewelry again. The beach was massive, the crowd had long since left, and even in the daylight, every bit of sand looked exactly the same.

"Next," I continued, "we pray."

She blinked. "Really?"

I nodded. "Yes. Sometimes when we don't know what else to do, we ask for help. Even if we're not sure who's listening."

Right there, in that noisy restaurant, we bowed our heads over a half-eaten plate of hush puppies.

"Dear God," I prayed quietly, "please help us find Julia's jewelry. We know it's just stuff, but it means a lot to her. And she did her best to keep it safe. If there's any way we can get it back, please guide us. Amen."

Julia opened her eyes and gave a small, uncertain nod. "Let's try."

The drive back to the beach was quieter than usual. The sun had dipped below the horizon, leaving a soft orange glow fading into twilight. Streetlights flickered on as we pulled into the familiar parking lot, now mostly empty except for a few late-night walkers and fishermen.

We grabbed a flashlight and made our way over the dune. The beach was a different world now—still, hushed, the sky above fading into indigo, and the crashing waves the only sound.

"Can you remember where we were?" I asked as we reached the sand.

Julia looked around slowly. She didn't answer right away. The wind tugged at her hair, and she hugged her arms to her chest.

"It all looks different now," she said finally. "But..."

She turned to the left, then took a few steps forward. Then a few more. I watched her, not wanting to interrupt whatever quiet intuition she was following. She was scanning the sand, looking not for a clear sign, but... something.

After about a minute of walking, she stopped and pointed. "There."

"Are you sure?"

"No," she admitted, "but... I just feel like it's here."

She got down on her knees and started brushing the sand away with her fingers. I knelt beside her, shining the flashlight to help. Grain by grain, she uncovered a corner of the blanket that must have been left behind, half buried in the sand.

She smiled. "This is it."

Julia dug carefully, her small hands moving with hope and precision. Within moments, her fingers curled around something metal.

Her dolphin necklace.

Then the ring.

Then the bracelet.

One by one, her lost treasures emerged, slightly gritty with sand but whole.

My mouth dropped open. "Julia! You found them!"

She nodded slowly, almost dazed. "I just... knew."

I sat back on my heels, heart full and stunned. "That beach is enormous," I said. "It's like finding a grain of rice in a sandbox."

"I didn't think I would," Julia said quietly, cradling her jewelry. "But I asked. And... I just felt like I should walk that way."

I looked up at the stars beginning to appear in the darkening sky. The waves continued to roll in, indifferent to our little miracle.

"Maybe there was an angel listening after all," I said softly.

Julia looked at me, eyes wide. "You think so?"

I smiled. "Well, if there was, he must really like you."

She grinned. "Thanks, Angel."

We walked back together across the sand, our feet sinking into the cool earth with every step. The beach, in its quiet stillness, felt almost sacred in that moment. Something ordinary had just turned extraordinary.

I still don't know if an angel guided her hands that night. Maybe Julia noticed some subtle sign—an old soda can in the sand, a certain shadow cast just right, or the whisper of a dune. Or maybe, just maybe, it was something greater. Something unseen. Something holy.

All I know is that she found what was lost.

And I believe, with all my heart, that someone helped her.

Chapter 2

Chapter Two -- I Do Believe

Little boy digging in a hole by the beach

T

he beach has always been a special place for our family—a sanctuary of sunshine, salty breezes, and the simple joy of being together. But it's also been the backdrop for more than one quiet prayer whispered into the sea air, especially when something precious has gone missing. Of all those moments, one stands out in my memory with a clarity that still makes me pause and smile.

It was a hot summer day on the Outer Banks of North Carolina, the kind of day when the sun seems determined to toast every shoulder it touches and the ocean roars with an open invitation to jump in. If you've ever been to the Outer Banks, you know how it is. The beaches stretch on forever, but somehow, every inch of sand is covered—blanket to blanket—with families, couples, and solo sun-seekers trying to soak in the magic of summer.

That morning, we claimed a modest patch of beach real estate between two colorful umbrellas and laid out our towels and chairs. Coolers were unpacked, flip-flops tossed aside, and the scent of sunscreen filled the air as we settled in for a day of surf and sun.

Julia, my daughter, was about ten at the time—a sweet, thoughtful girl with curly blonde hair and a quiet sense of responsibility well beyond her years. Before dashing into the waves with her boogie board under one arm, she paused beside me.

"Mom," she said, tugging on my arm, "I'm going to take off my jewelry. I don't want to lose it in the water."

Smart girl. I watched as she carefully removed her little silver dolphin necklace, a friendship ring she'd gotten for her birthday, and a tiny charm bracelet she'd picked out herself the week before. Each piece meant something to her—not expensive, but special.

"I'll put it right here," she said, and knelt at the edge of our blanket.

She scooped a shallow hole into the sand and tucked her treasures inside, then covered them back up with a practiced hand, patting it down and brushing a corner of the blanket just over the spot. "There," she said with a nod of satisfaction. "Safe and sound."

I smiled. "Good thinking, sweetheart. Let's just remember to grab it before we go."

And with that, she sprinted toward the water, her laughter joining the rhythm of the waves.

The day passed in a blur of sunscreen reapplications, sandy sandwiches, and collecting seashells in plastic buckets. We built lopsided castles, played frisbee near the shoreline, and laughed until our stomachs hurt. When the shadows grew longer and the sun softened into a golden hue, we packed up and headed into town for dinner—sandy, sun-kissed, and content.

It wasn't until we were seated at a casual seafood spot—cold drinks in hand, the smell of fried shrimp in the air—that I heard the dreaded two syllables.

"Uh-oh."

My fork paused halfway to my mouth. I turned and saw Julia, wide-eyed, pale, and frozen mid-thought. Her lips parted again, and this time her voice was quieter, hesitant.

"Mom... I left my jewelry at the beach."

For a second, we just stared at each other. I could see the re-alization washing over her, followed by the rising tide of panic.

"Oh no," she whispered, her voice trembling. "It's buried in the sand. We didn't go back for it. I forgot. I'm so sorry—what should I do?"

I reached over and took her hand, squeezing it gently. "First, take a deep breath," I said, trying to sound calm even though my mind was already calculating how unlikely it was we'd ever find that jewelry again. The beach was massive, the crowd had long since left, and even in the daylight, every bit of sand looked exactly the same.

"Next," I continued, "we pray."

She blinked. "Really?"

I nodded. "Yes. Sometimes when we don't know what else to do, we ask for help. Even if we're not sure who's listening."

Right there, in that noisy restaurant, we bowed our heads over a half-eaten plate of hush puppies.

"Dear God," I prayed quietly, "please help us find Julia's jewelry. We know it's just stuff, but it means a lot to her. And she did her best to keep it safe. If there's any way we can get it back, please guide us. Amen."

Julia opened her eyes and gave a small, uncertain nod. "Let's try."

The drive back to the beach was quieter than usual. The sun had dipped below the horizon, leaving a soft orange glow fading into twilight. Streetlights flickered on as we pulled into the familiar parking lot, now mostly empty except for a few late-night walkers and fishermen.

We grabbed a flashlight and made our way over the dune. The beach was a different world now—still, hushed, the sky above fading into indigo, and the crashing waves the only sound.

"Can you remember where we were?" I asked as we reached the sand.

Julia looked around slowly. She didn't answer right away. The wind tugged at her hair, and she hugged her arms to her chest.

"It all looks different now," she said finally. "But..."

She turned to the left, then took a few steps forward. Then a few more. I watched her, not wanting to interrupt whatever quiet intuition she was following. She was scanning the sand, looking not for a clear sign, but... something.

After about a minute of walking, she stopped and pointed. "There."

"Are you sure?"

"No," she admitted, "but... I just feel like it's here."

She got down on her knees and started brushing the sand away with her fingers. I knelt beside her, shining the flashlight to help. Grain by grain, she uncovered a corner of the blanket that must have been left behind, half buried in the sand.

She smiled. "This is it."

Julia dug carefully, her small hands moving with hope and precision. Within moments, her fingers curled around something metal.

Her dolphin necklace.

Then the ring.

Then the bracelet.

One by one, her lost treasures emerged, slightly gritty with sand but whole.

My mouth dropped open. "Julia! You found them!"

She nodded slowly, almost dazed. "I just... knew."

I sat back on my heels, heart full and stunned. "That beach is enormous," I said. "It's like finding a grain of rice in a sandbox."

"I didn't think I would," Julia said quietly, cradling her jewelry. "But I asked. And... I just felt like I should walk that way."

I looked up at the stars beginning to appear in the darkening sky. The waves continued to roll in, indifferent to our little miracle.

"Maybe there was an angel listening after all," I said softly.

Julia looked at me, eyes wide. "You think so?"

I smiled. "Well, if there was, he must really like you."

She grinned. "Thanks, Angel."

We walked back together across the sand, our feet sinking into the cool earth with every step. The beach, in its quiet stillness, felt almost sacred in that moment. Something ordinary had just turned extraordinary.

I still don't know if an angel guided her hands that night. Maybe Julia noticed some subtle sign—an old soda can in the sand, a certain shadow cast just right, or the whisper of a dune. Or maybe, just maybe, it was something greater. Something unseen. Something holy.

All I know is that she found what was lost.

And I believe, with all my heart, that someone helped her.

Chapter 3

Chapter Three - The Just-In-Time Beach Angel

Young woman in a doctor's office, with
an angel by her side

S ome people roll their eyes when you mention guardian angels. Others nod politely, not wanting to disagree but clearly not convinced. Me? I believe. Not because of something I read in a book or heard in a sermon, but because I've lived through moments where I *know*—deep in my heart—that someone beyond this world was watching over us.

One of those moments happened at the beach. Of course, it did. It always seems to be the beach for us. Maybe it's something about the sea breeze or the endless stretch of sand that makes heaven feel just a little bit closer.

This time, it involved my daughter Julia—not a little girl anymore, but twenty years old and every bit the capable, adventurous spirit she'd always been. We were on a family trip to the Outer Banks, our beloved vacation spot. You know the kind: sun-soaked afternoons, the scent of salt in the air, seashells in your pocket, and the sound of waves playing background music to everything you do.

On our second day, Julia mentioned that she had a rash. At first glance, it looked like a run-of-the-mill irritation, the kind you get from brushing against sea oats or a stray patch of poison ivy while walking the trails near the dunes.

She came into the kitchen rubbing her arm. "Mom, look at this. It's kind of itchy."

I peered at the red, blotchy skin. "Hmm. That could be poison ivy. Or some kind of contact rash. Calamine lotion should help." I grabbed the familiar pink bottle from the travel bag and handed it over. "And don't forget to drink lots of water," I added, wagging my finger in mock seriousness. "You always feel better when you're hydrated."

Julia rolled her eyes, smiling. "You and your water advice."

"Hey, clean skin and hydration never hurt anyone. It's like armor for the modern age."

We both laughed, and she went to apply the lotion. But that night, as the moon rose over the ocean and the waves rolled gently under a star-strewn sky, things started to change.

Early the next morning, just as the sun was beginning to break across the horizon, Julia tapped on my bedroom door.

"Mom?" Her voice was soft and shaky.

I sat up immediately. "What's wrong?"

She stepped into the room, and I could see it even in the dim light—her arms, her chest, her neck. The rash wasn't just worse. It was everywhere. Her skin was angry, red, and swollen, and her eyes held something deeper than discomfort: fear.

"Something's really wrong," she whispered.

That was all I needed to hear. I grabbed my keys and my purse, and within five minutes, we were driving toward the medical clinic.

Now, the Outer Banks clinic is the go-to spot for every sunburn, sting, and sprain from Corolla to Hatteras. And being a Monday morning in peak vacation season, it was—of course—packed. We signed in, found two seats near the back of the waiting room, and waited.

At first, we tried to distract ourselves. I pulled out my phone. Julia leaned her head against the wall, trying to breathe through the itching. But as we waited, I could *see* the rash spreading—right before my eyes.

"Is it just me," I asked quietly, "or is that creeping up your neck?"

Julia pulled out her phone and flipped to her front camera to check. "Yep," she muttered. "My legs, too."

"Okay, we're definitely getting a nurse the next time someone walks by."

"I feel like a walking science experiment," she groaned, scratching her forearm.

"You're going to be fine," I said, trying to sound calm. "We just need to get you in front of a doctor."

After about an hour of watching the rash march across her body like an invading army, Julia finally walked up to the reception desk.

"Hi," she said, trying to stay composed, "I really think I need to be seen soon. My rash is spreading really fast, and I don't feel right."

The receptionist barely looked up. "We're helping everyone as quickly as we can. Please take a seat."

Julia turned and gave me a half-smile as she returned to her chair.

"I tried."

"I saw," I said, squeezing her hand. "We'll wait just a bit longer, but if anything changes, we go back up."

That "bit longer" turned out to be thirty more minutes. And then, finally, they called her name.

I stayed behind in the waiting room, relieved that help was finally coming. I scrolled on my phone, prayed quietly under my breath, and kept glancing toward the hallway.

Ten minutes later, the nurse stepped out and called my name. "You can come back now. The doctor asked for you."

There was something in her tone—something tight, urgent—that made my heart skip.

I followed her down the hall and into the small exam room. Julia was sitting on the exam table, red-faced and gripping the edge of the seat. The doctor stood beside her, holding a stethoscope and a blood pressure cuff.

"Her throat's swelling," the doctor said to me without preamble. "We're administering antihistamines and steroids now."

Julia turned her eyes toward me. They were wide with panic. "Mom... it's getting harder to breathe."

My heart dropped.

"Hang in there, baby," I said, brushing her hair back. "You're going to be okay."

I watched as the doctor moved quickly, giving the injection and barking instructions to the nurse. Every second felt like an hour. Julia gasped once, then coughed, and for one terrifying moment, I thought she would stop breathing altogether.

Then—like someone had flipped a switch—she began to settle. Her breaths became less shallow. The redness in her face softened. Her eyes, though still wet with tears, looked more alert.

"She's stabilizing," the doctor said. "That was very close."

I didn't know whether to cry or collapse. I just reached for Julia's hand and held on tight.

Later, when we were in the car, heading slowly back to the beach house, I kept thinking about how close it had been. Five more minutes. Just five more minutes in that waiting room, and she might not have made it back to the exam room in time.

And that thought—it haunts me.

"I think I had an angel today," Julia said softly, watching the ocean blur past the window.

I glanced at her. "I think you did too."

"Just in time," she whispered.

"Just in time," I repeated.

That wasn't the last time we saw this mysterious allergy show up. A few months later, at home, it struck again—fast, furious, and terrifying. This time, we called 911 immediately. An ambulance rushed her to the hospital, and once again, she was saved.

To this day, we never found out what caused it. No clear trigger. No diagnosis that stuck. Just a sudden, severe reaction and a few unforgettable brushes with danger.

Julia now carries an epi-pen in her purse. She doesn't leave home without it. And she always keeps a water bottle with her—just to make her mother smile.

But more than anything, she carries something else. A deep, unshakable sense that someone is watching over her. That someone showed up not once, but twice, in the exact moment she needed saving.

We've come to call it her "Just-In-Time Angel." The one who helped her when seconds mattered.

And me? I thank God for that angel every time I look at my daughter.

Because I believe.

Chapter 4

Chapter Four - Guardian Angels – Everyone Has One

Angel carrying a gas can to a car on the
side of the road

It's easy to think of guardian angels as the quiet protectors of children—hovering above little heads during scraped knees and bike crashes. But I've come to believe, with every fiber of my being, that everyone has a guardian angel. Not just the young or the reckless. Even our parents. Even—especially—our so-called "golden agers."

Take, for instance, this unforgettable story starring my own parents.

They were both in their sixties at the time, healthy, sharp, and still fond of doing things their own way. Every year, like clockwork, they'd make their annual pilgrimage from their home in Cleveland, Ohio to visit us in northern Virginia. It was a tradition we all loved—one that meant laughter, shared meals, walks around the lake, and inevitably, the telling of old stories that never failed to make us laugh.

That year, however, the story didn't wait until they arrived. It unfolded on the way—and it reminded us all just how real divine protection can be.

The day had started out fine. They were packed, the house was locked up, and my dad, ever the designated driver, had mapped out the route. My mom, as usual, brought along a well-organized cooler and a magazine.

Somewhere along the way—perhaps around West Virginia—my mom glanced at the dashboard and noticed something was wrong.

"Steve," she said cautiously, "didn't we pass our normal gas station about twenty miles ago?"

My father didn't look up. "Yep."

"You didn't stop."

"Didn't need to," he replied casually, tapping the wheel with his fingers. "We're good for a while."

Mom raised an eyebrow but went back to her magazine. For the next half-hour, she didn't say anything. But every few exits, she glanced at the gas gauge. Each time, the needle crept lower. Still, Dad remained as unbothered as ever.

Finally, unable to stay silent, she said, "Steve, the gauge is getting awfully close to empty."

He gave her a familiar look—the one that said, *I've been driving longer than you've been worrying.* "It's okay."

She let it go. For about ten more miles.

"Steve, it says 'LOW GAS'. The light is blinking!"

He glanced at the dashboard. "Still okay."

"Are you waiting for it to shout at us?"

"It's fine. I know this car."

"You also thought you knew the way to Karen's house in 1989 and ended up in Roanoke," she muttered.

"Still got us there," he said with a chuckle.

But as the miles rolled by, the blinking light became harder to ignore. Mom shifted uncomfortably in her seat. "Steve, please pull off. Just find the next exit."

"Alright, alright," he sighed. "I'll get off at the next ramp."

A few tense minutes later, the off-ramp appeared like a shimmering mirage, and Dad took it—just in time. As they crested the rise and started their descent, the car sputtered, coughed, and rolled to a stop just as they reached the shoulder.

My dad turned the key again. Nothing.

"Out of gas," he said, more surprised than concerned.

"I *told* you," Mom said, her voice now tinged with both exasperation and anxiety.

She looked around. No gas station in sight. Just a long, empty stretch of road flanked by trees, the late afternoon sun casting long shadows across the landscape. Cars zoomed past them at regular intervals, none stopping. Her fingers tightened around her seatbelt.

"I'm saying the Our Father," she announced, folding her hands.

My dad raised his eyebrows. "It's not that bad."

"It could have been worse," she muttered. "What if this had happened on the highway? What if it's hours before someone stops? What if we have to walk?"

"Then we walk. Or flag someone down."

"In this heat? On the side of the road?"

He was about to answer when the rumble of an approaching vehicle caught their attention. A pickup truck slowed as it neared them. Its turn signal flashed, and it pulled onto the shoulder just behind their car.

Both of my parents turned to look. A man in his late forties climbed out. He wore jeans, work boots, and a well-worn baseball cap. His face, weathered but kind, broke into a friendly smile.

"Y'all run outta gas?" he asked, approaching the window.

Dad rolled it down. "Yeah. I ignored my wife's warnings and now here we are."

The man chuckled. "Happens more than you'd think."

"We're trying to get to northern Virginia," Mom added. "Do you know if there's a station nearby?"

"There is," the man nodded. "About five miles that way." He gestured with his thumb over his shoulder. "But you're not going to make it walking."

He walked back to his truck and opened the bed. A moment later, he returned holding a red gas can.

"I always keep a spare," he said, unscrewing the cap. "You'd be surprised how many folks I've helped with this."

He poured the gas into their tank as my parents looked on in stunned silence.

"That should be enough to get you to the station," he said. "I'll follow you there just to be sure."

Mom blinked. "You don't have to do that."

"I don't mind. Got nowhere to be until dinner. Besides," he added with a grin, "you've got good guardian angels."

My dad laughed. "Seems like they sent you."

The man tipped his cap. "I'm happy to help."

True to his word, he followed them all the way to the small gas station five miles down the road. Once there, Dad filled the tank and then insisted on refilling the man's gas can.

"Least we can do," he said.

The man gave a friendly wave and climbed back into his truck. They watched as he pulled away, disappearing into the stream of traffic.

And just like that, he was gone.

Mom stood beside the car, her hand resting on the passenger door. She looked over at Dad.

"I mean it, Steve. That was an angel."

He smiled at her. "A gas-pumping, truck-driving angel?"

She nodded firmly. "Exactly. Right place, right time. What else do you call that?"

He wrapped his arm around her shoulders. "A lucky break."

She rolled her eyes. "You can call it luck. I'll call it divine intervention. Either way, I'm saying one more 'Thank You' prayer."

They made it to my house that evening just after sunset, tired but safe. When I opened the door, Mom greeted me with a hug and immediately launched into the story—hands flying, eyes wide, her voice animated.

"And he just *had* gas, Karen. Can you believe that? He had a full can in the back of his truck. Who even does that these days?"

"I told her," Dad said behind her, "it was fine."

"And I told him *God was watching*," Mom finished.

We laughed, hugged, and sat down to dinner. But that story stayed with me.

It still does.

Because it was more than a feel-good tale. It was a reminder—subtle but powerful—that no matter your age, no matter your plans, no matter your stubbornness—there's always someone looking out for you. Someone who shows up in the nick of time, often dressed in jeans and kindness, ready to lend a hand.

Even golden agers have guardian angels.

Maybe especially them.

Chapter 5

Chapter Five - Some People Learn The Hard Way

Car in the middle of a road, almost to
the gas station

There's a reason people say, *"Don't try this at home."* And in my case, I say it with conviction—because, naturally, I *did* try it.

This story begins the way many adventures do: with good intentions and poor judgment. It was just me and my eight-year-old son, David, making our usual drive from Ohio to northern Virginia. We'd done the trip enough times for it to feel familiar, almost routine. But this time, the sun was already setting by the time we hit the road.

I had hesitated about leaving so late. It was bordering on nighttime, and the idea of driving on roads after dark with a sleepy child in the backseat wasn't exactly in the *Responsible Parenting* handbook. Still, the bags were packed, the snacks were stashed, and my determination was strong. We'd get a head start on traffic and make decent time, I thought. After all, what could possibly go wrong?

The first few hours were uneventful. The radio hummed softly with oldies, and David had curled up in the back seat with a pillow and his well-loved stuffed bear, dozing peacefully as the mile markers passed in a blur of headlights and shadows.

Somewhere near the state border, I noticed the traffic on the turnpike coming to a near standstill. I frowned at the sight of brake lights stretching endlessly ahead and made a snap decision.

"Let's take a different way," I said aloud to myself, though David was sound asleep. I glanced at my GPS. There was a relatively new highway that would cut through some of the congestion and save us time. A little detour never hurt anyone, right?

I veered off the turnpike and onto the alternate route, patting myself on the back for being clever. It wasn't long before we were cruising down the quiet, two-lane highway under a blanket of stars. The road was smooth, the traffic was light, and all seemed well—until I looked at the gas gauge.

It hovered just above a quarter tank.

Now, anyone who's ever driven knows that the first three-quarters of a gas tank seem to last for *hours*. But that last quarter? It vanishes faster than a cookie in a kindergarten class.

I considered pulling off at the next exit, but then I looked at David's peaceful face in the rearview mirror. Waking him up would be like releasing a wild animal—he'd be disoriented, grumpy, and instantly craving a bathroom break, a juice box, possibly a toy, and definitely ice cream. I wasn't ready to deal with that just yet.

So, I made the only *reasonable* decision.

I kept driving.

Just a little farther, I reasoned. There had to be a gas station coming up soon. Besides, the light hadn't come on yet. I still had time.

Fifteen minutes later, the gas light blinked on.

I sighed. "Okay, okay. I get it," I muttered to the dashboard. "We need gas."

Now fully committed to this risky choice, I started taking exits whenever I saw a sign that promised gas nearby. But one by one, the stations turned out to be closed—shuttered for the night, dark as the sky above us.

And unlike the trusty turnpike rest stops—those blessed oases of 24-hour convenience—this new highway didn't offer much in the way of civilization. It was just road. Long, dark, lonely road. With every exit I took, I burned more gas. With every mile, I began to worry just a little more.

Still, I wasn't panicking. Not exactly.

Something in me felt... calm. Strange, isn't it? I wasn't making wise choices, but I had this quiet certainty that somehow, things would work out.

Maybe that was faith.

Or maybe that was my guardian angel doing overtime.

The digital clock on the dashboard blinked **12:06 AM** as I passed into West Virginia. The roads were emptier than ever, and my gas gauge now flirted with the "E" line like a tightrope walker leaning too far.

And then, like something out of a movie, I saw it.

Neon lights.

Bright red, glowing against the black sky like a lighthouse for the weary and the nearly stranded.

TRUCK STOP – OPEN 24 HOURS

I nearly wept with joy.

"Hang on, David," I said, as if he could hear me through his sleep. "We're almost there."

I turned off the highway and eased onto the off-ramp, the car coasting like it too was relieved to have made it this far. But, as fate would have it, about 50 yards from the entrance, the car sputtered.

And died.

David stirred in the backseat. "Why are we stopping?" he mumbled, groggy.

"The car just needs a nap," I said with a smile. "We're really close."

I turned the key. Nothing. I tried again, this time pressing the brake and praying. Still nothing.

Then I remembered something—an old trick my dad once taught me.

"If the car's on an incline," he'd said, "the gas might shift just enough to help it start."

I looked around. Sure enough, we were parked at a slight angle. I took a breath, turned the key again—

VROOOM.

The engine roared to life.

"Yes!" I shouted. David sat up straighter.

"Are we moving now?"

"Yep. We're going to get gas, buddy. Everything's okay."

We pulled up to the pump, and I didn't even mind that only the high-test premium was available. I would've paid double just to get us rolling again.

After filling the tank, I let David pick out a snack. Naturally, he chose ice cream.

"It's past midnight, you know," I said, raising an eyebrow.

"Isn't that the best time for ice cream?" he grinned.

I laughed. "Tonight, you win."

As we sat on the curb, licking our cones under the humming truck stop lights, the moment felt surreal. Like a dream. Except I knew it wasn't.

It really happened.

And I will forever be grateful for the unseen hand that nudged us forward when things could have easily gone the other way.

I sometimes wonder—what if that truck stop hadn't been there? What if we had broken down just a few miles back, in the middle of nowhere, with no lights, no gas, no help?

But we didn't.

We made it.

Because someone was watching.

Chapter 6

Chapter Six - A Grandmother's Prayer is Answered

Older woman cradling a baby

The year was 1982. Big hair, cassette tapes, and rotary phones were still a thing. And somewhere on the other side of the globe, my husband—an Air Force officer—was stationed in Korea, serving his country. Meanwhile, back in the United States, I was eight months pregnant, chasing after a very energetic 18-month-old daughter, and living in a suburb of Washington, D.C., far from my family and most familiar comforts.

To be exact, I was living in Virginia, and my only nearby relatives were my husband's brother and sister-in-law. My sister-in-law, thankfully, happened to be a neonatal nurse—a gift from above if ever there was one. With my due date quickly approaching, we crafted what we believed was a well-thought-out labor and delivery plan.

The Plan:

1. I would go into labor.
2. When contractions became seven minutes apart, I would call my sister-in-law.
3. She would drive to my house in *her* car (a vehicle we all silently prayed would actually start).
4. Then, she would drive *me* to the hospital using *my* car (a much newer, more reliable vehicle).
5. My mom, who had flown in from Ohio to help, would stay behind to watch my toddler.

Simple. Logical. Foolproof.
Almost.
There was one tiny, not-so-insignificant detail that haunted the back of my mother's mind: what if my Mom had to drive me to the hospital. To make matters worse, **my car was a manual transmission.** And while I felt confident handing over the keys if needed, my mother hadn't driven a stick shift in over **twenty years**. Combine that with the looming possibility of

her needing to drive a laboring daughter and a confused toddler across the *Washington Beltway* at rush hour, and, well—you can understand why she was quietly having heart palpitations.

And so, she did the only thing she knew to do: **she prayed.**

She prayed fervently. She prayed daily. She prayed like a mother who *really* didn't want to stall in third gear while navigating D.C. traffic with her daughter in full-blown labor.

"Lord," she whispered during her morning coffee. "Please don't let me have to drive that car. Or this woman. Or her toddler. Or do *any* of that. Amen."

As the days passed, I waddled through the last weeks of pregnancy. My daughter stayed glued to my hip, completely unaware of the life change about to rock her world. My mother tiptoed around the house trying to stay calm, but I caught her sneaking glances at my car's gearshift more than once with visible dread on her face.

Then it happened.

It was around **1:45 AM**, early one morning when everything was still and the world felt paused. I felt a sudden contraction. Then another. Not five minutes apart, not three minutes—but back-to-back, fast, intense, and followed immediately by the unmistakable *whoosh* of my water breaking.

I called out, my voice echoing down the hallway, "Mom? MOM! I don't think I'm going to make it to the hospital!"

There was a rustling of sheets, a thud as she knocked into something in the dark, and then her voice from the other room: *"Karen, what have you gotten me into now?"*

She bolted into the bathroom, took one look at me and the soaked floor, and went into emergency grandma mode. She grabbed the phone and called the hospital. As she was being transferred to a nurse, she kept poking her head back into the bathroom.

"She says she doesn't think she's going to make it to the hospital," Mom told the nurse breathlessly. "And—I think she's right!"

The nurse on the other end stayed calm, talking Mom through what to expect. Meanwhile, I was now sitting on the floor of the bathroom—thankfully spacious—and bracing against the vanity with one hand while the other clutched a towel.

"I think... I think she's coming!" I gasped.

The nurse's voice, filtered through the corded phone, said calmly, "Can you see the baby's head?"

Mom leaned in. "Oh, dear Lord, yes!"

The next few minutes were a blur. My mother—God bless her—was hopping between me and the phone, trying to relay what was happening while staying composed. The nurse stayed on the line, guiding her through it. There were no contractions to count anymore. There was no time for precision or plans.

Then, with a cry that filled the bathroom and every corner of my soul, **my baby girl was born.**

Tiny. Beautiful. Alive.

And right there on the bathroom floor.

I held her to my chest, shaking from adrenaline, tears streaking down my face. Mom dropped the phone, knelt beside me, and placed her hands gently on both of us. "She's crying. That's a good sign," she whispered.

We didn't need medical degrees to know that everything was okay in that moment.

Then, Grandma sprang into action again. She called **my sister-in-law** and then **911**.

The next act in this miracle comedy was my sister-in-law's dramatic arrival.

After hearing that I was *actually giving birth*, she threw on her clothes and flew down the highway, pushing her aging sedan to the limit. She later confessed to running every red light and talking to God the whole way. "Just hold on, Lord. Please let me get there."

She arrived seconds after the paramedics pulled in, slammed the gearshift into park, and the car—quite literally—*died*. Engine off. Completely unresponsive. As if the vehicle had said, "This was my last mission. Goodbye."

She ran inside just as the EMTs were checking on me and the baby. "I'm here! Is she okay? Oh my gosh—*you did it?!*"

"I had help," I said, nodding toward Mom, who was now holding my toddler in her arms.

Speaking of which, my 19-month-old had awakened somewhere during all the chaos. She peeked out from the living room doorway, rubbing her eyes.

"Your mommy is very busy," Grandma told her gently. "You just sit here and be very quiet, okay?"

And Barbara did. Like she *knew*. Like some deep, unspoken child instinct told her that this was one of those rare, life-changing moments—and that the best thing she could do was sit still and let it unfold.

The paramedics examined me, checked the baby, and declared both of us stable. One looked at me and said with a smile, "Well, looks like this little one was in a hurry to meet you."

Then came the part I'll never forget. Since this was a clear emergency, they took us to the **nearest** hospital—three minutes away—*not* the military one we were supposed to use, which was over 45 minutes away. And thank heaven for that. I truly don't think I could've made the trip.

My sister-in-law rode with me in the ambulance, holding my hand the whole time. She read every expression on my face and reassured me over and over. "I'm right here. I won't leave. I'll watch the baby while they tag her and make sure she stays with you."

I can't express how much that meant to me. Her presence, her calmness, her confidence. After the whirlwind that had just occurred, it was like a grounding force—an answered prayer in itself.

Hours later, resting in a hospital bed with my new baby snuggling beside me, I exhaled deeply for the first time. My mother visited, now visibly relaxed for the first time in days.

"I told you I prayed," she said, patting my arm.

"Well, I'd say your prayer got a very dramatic answer."

She smiled. "God knows I meant it. I couldn't have driven that stick shift if my life depended on it."

And she didn't have to.

Epilogue

A few days later, the Red Cross delivered the news to my husband in Korea: *"You have a baby girl. She was born at home!"*

To which he reportedly replied, "That wouldn't have happened if I'd been there!"

Of course not. Because everything always goes according to plan when the men are involved—right?

We let them believe that.

Chapter 7

Chapter Seven - The Call Heard 400 Miles Away!

Old man resting in a chair, with an angel lingering behind.

I've never been quite sure where the line lies between divine intervention and coincidence. Whether it's saints quietly walking among us, angels gently guiding us, or the unmistakable hand of God shaping events behind the scenes—there are just some moments in life that defy explanation.

This is one of those moments. And it still gives me chills when I think about it.

It was a crisp autumn weekend in Virginia, and the house was already humming with quiet activity by the time the sun peeked over the horizon. My life was full at the time—soccer games, laundry, parenting, errands. You know the kind of days that seem to run before your feet hit the floor.

But this story starts just before that kind of busyness.

It was a Saturday morning, and the time was **exactly 5:00 AM**.

I was pulled out of sleep by a sound—no, a voice.

My father's voice.

It was unmistakable. Not just a memory or a distant echo, but *clear and real,* as if he were standing at the foot of my bed.

"Karen."

Just that. Just my name, spoken in the same calm but purposeful tone he used when I was a child and he'd call me down from my upstairs bedroom. It wasn't loud. It wasn't panicked. It wasn't even alarming. It was... familiar. Personal. Filled with something that, in retrospect, I would call *urgency wrapped in love.*

I sat up, heart pounding.

Beside me, my husband stirred. "What's wrong?" he mumbled, rubbing his eyes.

"I—I just heard my Dad," I whispered, staring at the darkened corner of the room. "He called me. I swear I heard him."

He sat up slightly. "Here? In the house?"

"No. Not here. But it was his voice. Like he was calling me from the other room. Like when I was little."

He blinked, processing. "Maybe it was a dream?"

"I don't think so," I said slowly. "It felt real."

We sat there in silence, both trying to make sense of it.

"Should I call?" I asked hesitantly. "It's five in the morning..."

He shrugged, half-asleep again. "If you're worried, maybe just wait a bit. It might've just been a dream, babe."

I nodded, but something gnawed at me. A restlessness in my chest. My father lived over **400 miles away** in Ohio, and though I had no reason to believe anything was wrong, my gut told me otherwise.

Still, I didn't call.

Morning crept in, and soon I was swallowed by the demands of a Saturday. Soccer cleats and shin guards, grocery lists and loads of laundry. I moved from task to task, trying to shake the eerie feeling, but my dad lingered in the back of my mind.

I thought of him often that day. Not just passingly, but deeply—moments flashing in my mind: him laughing in the backyard while grilling, his hands steady as he helped me with my science project, the way he always accepted gifts with genuine wonder, even if it was a tie that looked like six others he already owned.

My dad was a man of few words, but his love didn't require grand speeches. It was in his hugs. His quiet pride. His dependable presence.

And, as I'd learned in recent years, his strength.

He'd started having **minor strokes** a few years before. Nothing that kept him from working, at least not at first. With medication and regular check-ups, he managed to live a relatively normal life all the way through to retirement. He didn't complain. He didn't like to cause worry. That was just who he was.

But the voice I heard that morning wasn't casual. It didn't feel like nothing.

And then Sunday came.

That afternoon, my phone rang. It was my mother.

Her voice was calm, but there was something tight beneath the surface.

"Karen," she began, "I just wanted to let you know... your dad had a stroke yesterday."

I froze. "Yesterday? What time?"

"Early. Around five in the morning."

My breath caught. I felt like someone had knocked the wind out of me.

"I—Mom—I heard him," I stammered. "I heard his voice at that exact time. He called my name. I thought it was a dream..."

She paused. "You *heard* him?"

"I swear it," I whispered. "He called me. It was just like when I was a kid."

There was silence on the other end, as if she didn't know how to respond.

"Well," she said finally, "I think that must've been your dad's guardian angel—or maybe yours."

She went on to explain what had happened. My father had suffered a **massive stroke**—not the small ones that had been troubling him before, but something far more serious.

He had collapsed in his favorite chair in the living room. My mom and my brother had been nearby, watching him, unsure of what was happening. He wasn't unconscious exactly, but he wasn't responsive either.

"We weren't sure at first what to do," she admitted. "We kept hoping he'd come around."

They waited, uncertain, and time ticked by. Eventually, they took him to the hospital, but not until much later in the day. Between dealing with doctors, coordinating care, and simply trying to understand what was happening, calling me didn't even cross their minds until the next morning.

"You didn't call me because you didn't want to worry me," I said, a mix of sadness and frustration tightening my throat.

"We didn't want to disturb you unless we knew how serious it was," she replied gently. "And it was just so much all at once."

I understood. But still, I couldn't shake the thought: what if I had called? What if I had been able to talk to him, to comfort him, to urge them to take him in sooner?

But I hadn't.

Instead, I got a different kind of call—a call of the soul, a voice echoing 400 miles through the silence of dawn, delivered not by phone, but perhaps by heaven itself.

I cried quietly that night. For what might have been. For what was. For the mysterious connection between a father and daughter that could not be broken by time or distance—or even the failing of the body.

But here's the best part of the story:

My dad recovered.

Not perfectly. He had a slight limp that never quite went away. But he came back to us—smiling, hugging, quietly soaking in life with the same grateful heart he always had.

He never spoke of calling out that morning. But he *smiled* when I told him what I'd heard. Just smiled and nodded.

"Sounds like something I'd do," he said softly, his hand warm in mine.

And I like to believe that somehow—*somehow*—he did.

Chapter 8

Chapter Eight - More Long-distance Communication

Middle aged woman sitting next to a telephone, with an angel looking on.

Love doesn't stop when breath does. It reaches, transcends, and sometimes—if we're lucky—it even calls.

My uncle had always been a quiet, thoughtful man, with the kind of steady presence that made you feel safe just being around him. He was never one for grand speeches or dramatic displays, but his love for his family, especially his wife of over fifty years, was deep, abiding, and unwavering. His wife—my Aunt Gladys—knew this more than anyone.

For several years, my uncle had been fighting cancer. It began slowly, with routine checkups, treatments, and hopeful outlooks. But as time went on, the disease pressed forward. Still, he kept his sense of humor and quiet grace, never complaining, always more worried about others than himself.

Eventually, when the doctors could do no more, he was moved to a hospice facility. It was a peaceful, sunlit place tucked into a quiet neighborhood, where the air seemed stiller, as if even the wind knew it had to tread softly. Aunt Gladys rarely left his side, sitting with him for hours each day, holding his hand, reading aloud, brushing the hair from his forehead, and talking softly—even when he grew too weak to respond.

On one of those long afternoons, as the shadows stretched long across the floor, they shared a moment I will never forget—though I wasn't there to witness it, I've heard the story so many times that I can almost see it.

My uncle had opened his eyes, faint but clear, and looked over at his wife.

"Gladys," he said with a faint smile, "when I get to the other side, I'll call you."

She blinked, surprised by the strength in his voice. "You'll... call me?"

"Yes," he replied, his lips curving upward, "just to let you know I got there safely."

She chuckled, shaking her head. "How are you going to call me from heaven, exactly?"

He winked. "Don't worry. I know the number."

Aunt Gladys laughed through her tears. "Well, just make sure you don't call during the news."

"I'll be careful," he whispered, squeezing her hand.

That was the kind of man he was—gentle, reassuring, even in the face of the unknown.

The next evening, after another long day spent by his side, Aunt Gladys finally went home to rest. The nurses had promised to call if there was any change. Her son and daughter-in-law had agreed to stay behind for a while longer. Reluctantly, she left the room, kissed his forehead, and whispered, "You call me, okay?"

He didn't respond. His eyes remained closed, his breathing shallow, but steady.

Back at home, she changed into her nightgown, made a cup of tea, and sat quietly in the living room. The house was filled with silence—thick, heavy, expectant. After a while, she lay down, the soft hum of the bedside clock the only sound in the room.

An hour passed.

Then the phone rang.

The shrill ring cut through the stillness, startling her upright.

She reached for the phone with trembling hands and brought the receiver to her ear.

"Hello?" she said, her voice shaky but hopeful.

Silence.

There was no voice, no static, no click. Just... nothing.

She held her breath, listening harder.

"Hello?" she tried again.

But the line was dead. Or at least, silent.

She stayed there for a moment, phone still pressed to her ear, a strange calm flooding through her. She couldn't explain it, but it was as if something had settled into her chest—something warm, certain, and profoundly peaceful.

She hung up the phone slowly, then sat back in the dark room, whispering, "Thank you."

The next morning, her daughter-in-law called.

"Mom," she began softly, "he passed last night."

Aunt Gladys's breath caught. "What time?"

There was a pause.

"Around 11:20."

Aunt Gladys felt her knees weaken. "That's exactly when the phone rang."

A pause hung between them.

Then a breath. Then tears.

Later that day, she shared the story with the rest of us. Her voice was quiet, reverent, like someone trying to describe a dream too sacred to fully put into words.

"I know it sounds crazy," she said, "but I'm telling you—he called me. I know it. I felt it. That was our goodbye."

I believed her.

We all did.

The phone call never showed up in the logs.

No one else had called the house.

There was no voicemail, no trace of the number. My cousin checked, just to be sure. He even contacted the phone company. But there was nothing to find.

And still, we all knew the truth.

Some people believe heaven is unreachable. That it's a place far beyond our earthly grasp, behind clouds and veils and some-where "up there."

But I don't think so.

Sometimes, I believe heaven finds *us*—right where we are.

Through a whisper. A feeling. A dream. Or a silent ring that breaks through the stillness to say, *I'm okay. I made it. I didn't for-get you.*

My uncle kept his promise.
He knew the number.

Chapter 9

Chapter Nine - My Dad Says Goodbye

Old man, in a hospital bed, with his eyes closed, saying, "Happy Birthday"

Some bonds refuse to fade—even in the face of silence, distance, or the final breath.

In my life, I've witnessed moments that defy reason, logic, and the physical limitations we often place on reality. I've come to believe—whether through the quiet presence of guardian angels or divine orchestration—that love doesn't follow human rules. It lingers. It reaches. It *communicates*. And sometimes, it breaks through in the most astonishing of ways.

This is the story of one of those moments.

It was late September. In Virginia, the leaves were just beginning to blaze with autumn color, and my life was, as always, moving a mile a minute.

It was the week of my birthday. But this birthday week felt different.

I was turning another year older, yes, but my thoughts were fixed miles away in Ohio, where my father—my steady, kind-hearted, quiet hero—lay in a hospital bed, slowly slipping away from us.

He had been ill for some time. First the small strokes, then the gradual weakening of his body. My mother kept me updated as best she could, her voice composed but carrying a quiet tremble that told me all I needed to know.

"He's not in pain," she had said gently a few days earlier. "But... he's not really with us anymore. He just sleeps now, Karen. Eyes closed. Not speaking."

I knew then it was time.

I arranged to travel to Ohio the next day. It wasn't just about being present for his last moments—it was about *showing up* for a man who had never failed to do the same for me.

My father had always been a man of few words, but his love spoke volumes. I remember being a little girl, watching him accept gifts—no matter how big or small—with wide-eyed gratitude, as if someone giving him a pair of socks or a homemade card was the most touching gesture he'd ever seen. He didn't need much. Just family, his chair in the living room, and a good laugh at a corny joke.

He also had a nickname for me.

"Carin' for You."

It was a playful twist, a pun on "Karen-for-you," which he used to explain it with a twinkle in his eye. But it meant more than just a clever wordplay. It *was* his message—that he loved me deeply, unconditionally, and always.

The trip to Ohio was quiet. I drove on the turnpike, watching clouds drift by, trying to prepare myself for what I would find. But how do you prepare to say goodbye?

When I arrived at the hospital, the corridors felt colder than I remembered. The fluorescent lights overhead buzzed softly as my shoes squeaked down the polished floor. I paused just outside his room, bracing myself.

Inside, my father lay motionless.

His chest rose and fell in slow, measured breaths. His eyes were shut, his face pale but peaceful. Wires and machines surrounded him, beeping steadily—mocking the silence in the room.

My mom sat beside him, holding his hand. She looked up and offered me a tired smile.

"He's been like this for hours," she whispered. "Just resting."

I stepped to his bedside, suddenly overwhelmed by how small he looked beneath the crisp white hospital sheets. I reached out and brushed a hand over his, the familiar warmth of his skin strangely comforting.

"Hi, Dad," I said softly. "I'm here."

He didn't move.

My mom stood up and gently leaned over him. "Honey," she said in her softest voice, the one she used when coaxing a baby to sleep or soothing tears. "Karen's here. It's her birthday today."

And then—something happened.

Without warning, without fluttering his eyes open or adjusting his body, my father's lips began to move. Barely a whisper at first, but then more distinct, with the rhythm and melody I had memorized as a child.

"Happy birthday to you...
Happy birthday to you...
Happy birthday to my Carin' for you..."

Tears sprang instantly to my eyes.

He sang it like he had for years—warm and full of that unmistakable fatherly affection that makes you feel like the most loved person in the world.

I covered my mouth, my whole body trembling. "Dad," I choked, "you remembered."

And just like that, his lips fell silent again. His face relaxed. He slipped back into stillness, back into whatever place his mind and body had gone.

But he had come back. **For me.** For my birthday.

My mom pressed a tissue into my hand and wiped her own tears away.

"I haven't heard him speak in four days," she said, voice thick with emotion. "Four days, Karen. But he knew you were here. He knew it was you."

I could barely breathe. "I think... I think it was his angel. I think someone let him wake up just long enough to say goodbye."

She nodded. "He's always had a strong connection to you."

"Maybe it wasn't even goodbye," I whispered. "Maybe it was just... love."

The days that followed were slow and sacred.

I stayed close by. Held his hand. Talked to him. Read aloud from his favorite Bible verses and reminded him of old stories—how he'd taught me to ride a bike, how he never missed a school play, how he used to wait for me by the door when I came home from college with that a smile and open arms.

Though he never spoke again, I knew he was listening. I *felt* it.

When he finally passed, it was peaceful. Quiet. Just the way he would have wanted.

Even now, years later, I still think about that moment—his birthday song, whispered from the edge of this world into mine. I think about how impossible it seemed, how unlikely, how perfect.

How do you explain that kind of moment?

You don't.

You just hold it close and believe.

Chapter 10

Chapter Ten - And More Help From A Guardian Angel

Boys throwing candy at a car with an
angel in the background

A dolescence, as most parents will agree, is a uniquely unpredictable stage of life. It's full of hormones, sudden growth spurts, forgotten chores, half-eaten snacks in backpacks—and a general lack of something we grown-ups like to call *foresight*. At thirteen, my son was right in the middle of it. Smart and sweet, yes—but also impulsive, distractable, and, despite being just a seventh grader, already six feet tall.

He looked like a young man. But his decision-making capability, bless it, was still trying to catch up.

It was a bright, warm afternoon in early November—the kind of day that tricks you into thinking winter is still weeks away. The skies were cloudless, the sun slanting just right through the thinning trees, and the wind carried that distinct scent of dry leaves and cold air waiting just around the corner.

My son and a handful of his friends had walked down to the local 7-Eleven. It was a tradition they loved: pooling together spare change, laughing over choosing sodas and candy, and stretching the limits of their freedom just far enough to feel grown. That day, their treasure of choice was a box of **Jujubes**—those tiny, chewy, brightly-colored candies that stick to your molars like glue.

Walking back home with their haul, the boys were full of sugar and mischief, as boys so often are. And somewhere, right there on the sidewalk in our safe, quiet neighborhood, one of them had a "brilliant" idea.

"Hey," one of the boys said, holding up a bright green Jujube. "Bet I can hit that car."

The others laughed. Dared him. Then joined in.

Before long, those penny-sized candies were flying through the air at passing cars like brightly-colored confetti. They didn't throw them hard—Jujubes, after all, weigh about as much as a paperclip—but that didn't stop one driver from reacting.

Suddenly, a car jerked to a halt.

The laughter died instantly.

The doors flew open.

The passenger stepped out first—a large man, intimidating and furious, wearing a tangle of gold chains and covered in tattoos that snaked down his arms like angry vines. His entire presence screamed: **Do not mess with me.**

The boys scattered like birds startled by a thunderclap.

All except **my son**.

He froze.

I don't know why. Maybe he was stunned. Maybe he thought it wasn't that serious. Or maybe, standing there at six feet tall in a T-shirt and sneakers, the man mistook him for a much older teenager—or even an adult.

He didn't ask any questions. He didn't wait for an explanation.

He walked up to my son and began to **hit him**.

Hard.

Open-palmed smacks against the side of his head, so violent they echoed down the street. The blows came fast and fierce, until my son's knees gave way and he collapsed onto the pavement.

Then, just like that, the man turned and ran back to his car.

It sped off before anyone could get a license plate.

I wasn't there.

But the neighbors were.

They ran to help. Someone called 911. Paramedics arrived quickly and examined him at the scene.

"He's conscious," they said. "Vitals are stable. No visible wounds. Probably just stunned."

They brought him home, dazed and sore, but responsive. He was quiet—too quiet, even for him. When I asked what happened, he just blinked and muttered, "I don't know... it happened fast."

That night, he had a headache. Understandable, I thought.

The next day, it got worse.

And worse.

By the end of the week, the headaches were constant and severe. He winced at loud sounds, sat with his eyes half-shut, and rubbed his temples every few minutes. He couldn't remember where he put things. He struggled to finish sentences.

That's when I knew.

Something wasn't right.

We made an appointment. The doctor, kind and quick to act, sent us for a scan "just to be safe."

An hour later, she was back with the results, her face pale.

"There's bleeding," she said, carefully. "He has a fractured skull and a **subdural hematoma**—bleeding inside the brain. We're transferring him to **Children's Hospital** immediately."

My stomach dropped.

The car ride felt endless. My son leaned against the window, groaning softly, eyes fluttering shut every few minutes. I held his hand the whole time.

When we arrived, he was whisked away by a team of doctors. Children's was a teaching hospital, which meant we were quickly surrounded by a small army of residents, specialists, and students who looked at my son like he was a living, breathing textbook.

"He's an interesting case," one of them noted. "A child with a significant skull fracture and internal bleeding who remained functional for several days... quite rare."

The neurologist pulled me aside.

"Had he gone to sleep the night of the injury and not woken up, it wouldn't have surprised us," he said. "We may be looking at brain surgery."

I nodded, but everything around me felt like static. The idea of them cutting into my son's brain was too much to process.

HE stayed the night in the hospital. I barely slept. Every beep, every shift in his breathing jolted me awake. I prayed, quietly and constantly.

"Lord, I know I didn't get him here right away. I know this could've gone so wrong. But please... give him a chance. Don't let this be the end of his story."

The next morning, the doctors had more scans.

And then came the news that I can only describe as **a miracle**.

"The bleeding has slowed," the neurologist said. "The body is absorbing it. His skull is starting to heal on its own. No surgery for now."

My knees nearly gave out. "What?"

"He made it through the most critical hours. At this point, we're going to monitor. Let nature do its job."

I looked at my son—sleeping peacefully, his face relaxed for the first time in days—and whispered, "Thank you, God."

He had to visit the doctor's office for observation during the next week. During that time, he became a favorite among the nurses. Not because he was charming—though he was—but because he had learned all the cognitive tests by heart.

"Can you touch your nose with both index fingers?"

"Can you walk in a straight line with your eyes closed?"

"Can you remember this list of words?"

At some point, he looked at me and sighed. "Mom, I know them all. Can we just do them at home next time?"

Eventually, he was pronounced healed.

No surgery. No complications. No permanent damage.

Just **healing.**

Just a boy who was smacked hard enough to cause a brain bleed, but who, by the grace of God—and, I firmly believe, a **guardian angel**—survived.

Gratitude

I will never stop being thankful that:

- **He survived the first night**, when the bleeding could have taken him without warning.
- **No brain surgery was needed**, even though by all rights it should have been. (Yes, we didn't get him to the hospital soon enough—but maybe that's part of what saved him.)
- **His body healed**, guided by something bigger than medicine.

And above all...

- **His guardian angel was working overtime.**

I believe that with all my heart.

Chapter 11

Chapter Eleven - One More Happy Ending

Young boy on a skateboard, with an
angel watching

They say lightning doesn't strike the same place twice—but anyone who's raised a teenage boy knows that life doesn't always follow the rules of probability.

It was almost exactly one year after my son's terrifying injury—the skull fracture, the subdural hematoma, the near-miss that still echoed in my prayers—that we found ourselves, once again, staring danger in the face. This time, however, the culprit wasn't flying candy or a stranger's rage.

This time, it was a skateboard.

To be fair, I should have seen it coming.

My son had, in recent months, become entirely convinced that he was destined to become the next great skateboard legend. He watched videos endlessly—pros gliding up ramps, twisting mid-air, and landing with ridiculous grace, all set to the thump of techno music. And then, of course, he'd head outside and try to recreate every stunt on his own.

"Just watch, Mom," he told me proudly one Saturday morning, standing in the driveway with his board under one foot and a hoodie zipped halfway up. "I almost nailed a quarter loop yesterday."

"You almost *what*?" I blinked.

"It's like a half-pipe, but, you know, smaller. It's no big deal."

"Falling off the garage roof would also be no big deal?" I asked, my voice going up an octave.

He rolled his eyes. "I've got it under control."

I didn't press the point. You can't tell a 14-year-old anything when he's sure the world is watching him become famous.

And then came **Monday**—a school holiday, just like the one the year before.

I was inside folding laundry when I heard the crash.

That awful, sickening sound of something slamming hard against pavement, followed by silence.

Then: "MOM!!"

I dropped the clothes and ran outside.

He was on the ground, one leg awkwardly twisted, his skateboard halfway across the driveway. He clutched his ankle, his face pale and twisted in pain.

"What happened?!"

"I—I tried to go up the ramp. I flew off and—ugh—landed on my foot."

"Can you stand?"

"No. Definitely not."

I helped him inside, half-carrying him to the car while he groaned dramatically.

At the ER, we waited in the familiar hard plastic chairs, surrounded by the predictable murmur of coughs, shuffling nurses, and the distant beeping of machines.

Eventually, we were ushered in, and a doctor examined his ankle, then ordered x-rays.

The results came back relatively quickly.

"It looks like a very bad sprain," the doctor said, wrapping the ankle snugly. "Give it rest, keep it elevated, and use crutches. He should be up and moving in a couple of weeks."

Relieved, we went home, ice pack in hand and instructions neatly folded in a white envelope.

But my son wasn't convinced.

"I'm telling you," he said the next morning from the couch, "my ankle's broken."

"It's not," I said, setting down his glass of orange juice. "The x-ray showed a sprain. You heard the doctor."

"They missed it. I can feel it. It *cracks* when I move it."

"Well, stop moving it."

He glared. "I'm serious."

For the next two weeks, he refused to go to school.

"I can't walk on it."

"You have crutches."

"It hurts."

"It's a *sprain*."

"It's broken."

Eventually, he devised a method of getting around that was part brilliant, part ridiculous: he laid on his stomach on his skateboard and pushed himself down the hallway with his elbows.

I walked out of the kitchen one afternoon to see him gliding past with a bowl of cereal in one hand and a determined scowl on his face.

"You're going to scratch the floors," I said.

"Do you *want* me to walk?" he replied with a raised eyebrow.

"Touché."

And then came **the call**.

I was chopping vegetables for dinner when the phone rang. I wiped my hands and answered, expecting it to be the school or a telemarketer.

"Mrs. Shockley? This is Dr. Patel from the clinic. I wanted to follow up on your son's ankle."

"Yes?"

"Well, we've had another radiologist review the scans. It seems the original x-ray was a *wet read*, and unfortunately, those can sometimes obscure details. Upon closer inspection, it's clear your son actually suffered a *complete fracture* of the ankle."

My hand froze mid-air.

"A... what?"

"It was broken clean through," he said. "I'm so sorry it wasn't caught right away. We'd like you to bring him in as soon as possible so we can get him in a cast."

My mind spun. "Does he... need surgery?"

"That's what's remarkable," he continued. "Because the break wasn't diagnosed immediately, we didn't intervene. And yet somehow, he's been keeping his ankle at *precisely* the right angle for healing. It's aligned so perfectly, we don't need to reposition it. No surgery, no screws."

I looked across the room where my son was skateboarding belly-first toward the fridge.

"You don't say."

Back at the clinic, the doctor pulled up the scans and pointed to the screen.

"You see this?" he asked, highlighting a line so clean it looked like it had been drawn with a razor. "This is the fracture. If we'd seen it on the day of the injury, we likely would've scheduled surgery—pins, screws, the works."

My son looked up from the paper cup of water he was sipping. "But I'm good now?"

The doctor smiled. "You are. We'll fit you for a walking cast today, and you'll wear it for about four weeks. But the bone is already healing beautifully."

"So..." he grinned, "I was *right*?"

I sighed, rubbing my forehead. "Don't make me say it."

"You were right," the doctor said for me. "You knew something wasn't adding up. That kind of awareness is rare."

My son beamed. "See, Mom?"

At home, he took full advantage of his victory.

"Can I get a milkshake?"

"You have a broken ankle, not a broken blender."

"But my guardian angel says I deserve one."

I rolled my eyes. "Your guardian angel is going to need a raise."

As the days passed, his cast became a badge of honor.

He wrote messages on it. Drew cartoon characters. Had his friends sign it at school. He walked a little slower, took a few extra bathroom breaks, and milked it all for what it was worth.

And while I laughed along with him, deep down, I was filled with a strange, humbling kind of gratitude.

Because this could have gone so differently.

Had the bone shifted.

Had the swelling caused pressure.

Had we ignored his instincts completely.

But somehow, miraculously, everything aligned.

It's not often that you get a second chance in life without even realizing it. This wasn't just a story about a broken ankle. It was a reminder that, sometimes, **we are protected even when we don't know we need protecting.**

I had dismissed his instincts. I had trusted the original report. I had chalked up his complaints to drama.

And yet, something—or **someone**—guided him to hold his ankle *just so*, to move *just enough*, and to avoid the complications that so often come with misdiagnosed fractures.

Was it luck?

Maybe.

But I've come to believe in something greater.

Chapter 12

Chapter Twelve - Another Goodbye!

Woman holding a cell phone, with an angel behind her.

Goodbyes come in all forms. Some are long and tearful. Some are rushed and whispered. And some, as I've come to learn, are not spoken at all—but felt, sensed, and *received* in ways that no science or logic can explain.

This is one of those goodbyes. A quiet, mysterious, sacred farewell that came to me through a moment I will never forget.

It happened just two years after we met.

Mike and I were talking about marriage and planning a future together. We were in that beautiful, electric space between love and forever, where everything seems to sparkle just a bit more brightly. He was my best friend, my biggest cheerleader, my safe place in a world that could feel so loud.

It was a Tuesday afternoon when I spoke to him last. He called me from work.

"Hey, sweetheart," he said, his voice soft, a little strained.

"Hey, you," I replied, smiling automatically at the sound of his voice. "You don't sound so great."

"I'm not," he admitted. "I feel really off. Not sure what it is—just tired, kinda achy. I think I'm gonna head home early and lie down."

"Do you need me to come by?" I offered.

"No, no," he said quickly. "I think I just need to sleep it off. I'll be fine. I'll call you tomorrow."

"Okay," I said gently, though something in my gut felt uneasy. "Promise me you'll rest."

"I promise," he said, and I could almost hear him smile. "And hey—don't call tonight. I'm gonna try to sleep."

"All right," I said, reluctant. "Love you."

"Love you more."

We hung up.

That was the last time I heard his voice.

On Wednesday, I wanted so badly to call him. But his words echoed in my mind: *Don't call tonight.* I convinced myself that he was resting, that he'd wake up refreshed, maybe even laughing at how melodramatic he'd been.

I told myself this even as the knot in my stomach refused to go away.

Thursday morning came, and still—nothing. No text. No call. No funny meme sent to my inbox. The silence was getting louder.

I picked up the phone around noon and called.

No answer.

I called again. And again.

I left a voicemail. Then another.

Something was wrong.

That afternoon, I was in the car with a colleague, heading home after a long day. We chatted about traffic, about work, about what leftovers we were hoping to find in our refrigerators. But inside, I was distracted. My thoughts were back with Mike—my worry mounting with every passing minute.

And then my phone rang.

I glanced at the screen.

It was *Mike's number.*

A wave of relief washed over me.

"There he is," I said, half-laughing. "Finally!"

I held the phone in my hand for a moment. We were in a small car, and I didn't want to have a personal conversation with someone sitting just inches away. I figured I'd wait until I got home, find a quiet space, and then call him back.

After all, if he was calling, *he must be okay.*

That knowledge gave me a deep, unexpected peace. It was like warmth blooming in my chest. My body relaxed for the first time all day. I smiled out the window and felt a quiet thankfulness settle in my heart.

But that peace didn't last long.

Later that evening, just as I walked through my front door, my phone rang again. This time, it wasn't Mike's number. It was a mutual friend.

"Karen," he said, his voice flat, trembling. "I—I don't know how to say this."

My stomach dropped. "What? What is it?"

"It's Mike. He's... he's gone."

The words shattered something inside me.

"What do you mean gone?" I asked, my voice barely audible. "I just... I got a call from him this afternoon. He called me."

"No," the voice on the other end said, breaking. "He passed away Tuesday night. They found him this afternoon."

I collapsed onto the couch, unable to process the words.

"No," I whispered. "He called me. I *saw* his number."

But as I pulled up my call history, the screen told a different story.

There was *no call.*

No incoming call from Mike.

No missed call.

No voicemail.

I checked again. And again.

I called my brother in disbelief, desperate for an explanation, desperate for a glitch in the phone system that might account for what I *knew* I had seen.

He took my phone and looked at the log.

"There's nothing here," he said gently. "Karen... there's no call."

But there *was*. I *saw* it. I *felt* it. That moment in the car, the peace that filled my heart—it wasn't imagined. It was *real.*

Days passed. Then weeks.

I went through the motions of grief. The funeral. The cards. The long, sleepless nights and the tear-streaked days.

But through it all, I clung to that moment in the car.

Because deep down, I *knew* what it was.

It wasn't just a coincidence. It wasn't a dream or a trick of light or the mind trying to protect itself.

It was Mike.

He had come to say goodbye.

People often talk about "thin places"—those moments where the veil between this world and the next feels almost see-through. I think that Thursday afternoon was one of those moments for me.

I think that, somehow, he reached out. Maybe his soul knew that I needed peace, that I needed something to hold on to when the rest of the world began to fall apart.

And maybe, in his final act of love, he gave me that moment—quiet, comforting, unmistakable.

His goodbye kiss.

Chapter 13

The End

As I look back on this book and all of the memories it invokes, I now believe more strongly than ever that there are angels in this world that influence our lives. By accepting their existence, we can embrace their help and thank God for the gifts they are.

Review Guide

U se the following pages to review scripture verses and provide responses to the reflection questions.

Chapter 14

Chapter One Review

Luke 15:9-10 (KJV)
"And when she hath found it, she calleth her friends and her neighbours together, saying, Rejoice with me; for I have found the piece which I had lost.
Likewise, I say unto you, there is joy in the presence of the angels of God over one sinner that repenteth."

Reflection

In life, we lose things—small treasures, precious moments, even hope. But every lost thing matters to God. The story of Julia's buried jewelry is more than a tale of unlikely discovery. It's a quiet reminder that heaven notices even the smallest concerns we bring with open hearts.

When Julia paused to pray, it wasn't about the value of the jewelry. It was about the love behind it, the care she had taken to protect it, and the longing to be made whole again. And as she walked across that vast beach, guided by something deeper than memory, she found what was lost—just like the woman in Luke's parable.

Jesus tells us that the angels rejoice when what was lost is found. And sometimes, in moments just like this, we get a glimpse of that heavenly joy here on earth—a gentle answer, a whispered direction, a quiet miracle in the twilight.

Perhaps the beach became holy ground that evening—not because of what was found, but because of **who** was listening when you asked for help.

Chapter 15

Chapter Two Review

Psalm 91:11 (KJV)
"For he shall give his angels charge over thee, to keep thee in all thy ways."

Reflection

There are moments in life when protection comes in a way that defies explanation—when help arrives so swiftly, so precisely, that we are left wondering if heaven itself intervened. Psalm 91:11 reminds us that we are not alone on this journey. God, in His infinite love, appoints His angels to guard us, guide us, and yes, even rescue us when danger looms.

In this story, it wasn't just a man walking down the beach. It was a reminder that God sees us, hears our cries, and responds. Whether in the form of a stranger with strong arms or a whisper that tells us to buckle our seatbelt, His angels are real—and they are on assignment.

When we find ourselves overwhelmed or uncertain, let us rest in the promise that we are divinely watched over. And when deliverance comes, may we always have the faith to say, *"I do believe."*

Chapter 16

Chapter Three Review

Scripture Verse
Psalm 121:7-8 (KJV)
"The Lord shall preserve thee from all evil: he shall preserve thy soul. The Lord shall preserve thy going out and thy coming in from this time forth, and even for evermore."

Reflection

When life rushes in with unexpected danger, it's easy to feel overwhelmed and alone. But Psalm 121 reminds us that God's protection is not just passive—it's active, present, and persistent. He guards not only our lives, but our comings and goings, our most vulnerable moments, and even the steps we didn't realize were risky.

In Julia's case, God's timing was no accident. Help came at just the right moment, a whisper from heaven reminding us that we are seen, loved, and never alone. Guardian angels may wear many faces—doctors, nurses, strangers—but their mission is the same: to protect, to preserve, and to show us that God is always near.

Chapter 17

Chapter Four Review

Scripture Verse

Hebrews 13:2 (KJV)
"Be not forgetful to entertain strangers: for thereby some have entertained angels unawares."

Reflection

Guardian angels often don't come with wings or glowing halos. Sometimes they drive pickup trucks and carry gas cans. God's care for us is not limited by circumstance or age—He sends help in ordinary moments that become extraordinary through divine timing.

In a world filled with uncertainty, we can rest assured that our lives are not random. We are seen, known, and protected. Whether you're a young traveler or a seasoned couple on the road, your guardian angel is always on duty—watching, guiding, and sometimes, pulling up right behind you at just the right moment.

Chapter 18

Chapter Five Review

Scripture Verse

Psalm 46:1 (KJV)

"God is our refuge and strength, a very present help in trouble."

Reflection

Sometimes, trouble finds us not through catastrophe, but through small choices—late starts, ignored warning lights, or a sleepy child we hesitate to wake. And yet, even then, God's presence surrounds us. He doesn't always prevent the problem, but He always provides a path through it.

Whether it's a neon-lit truck stop appearing just in time or the quiet hum of a car engine roaring back to life, these moments are more than luck. They are reminders that we are never alone on the road. Our Guardian Angels are real, and they never sleep—even when we foolishly drive too far on too little gas.

Next time I'll plan better. But just in case, I'll still whisper a *thank you* to the One who always knows exactly where I am—even when I don't.

Chapter 19

Chapter Six Review

Scripture Verse

Philippians 4:6-7 (KJV)
"Be careful for nothing; but in every thing by prayer and supplication with thanksgiving let your requests be made known unto God.
And the peace of God, which passeth all understanding, shall keep your hearts and minds through Christ Jesus."

Reflection

God doesn't always follow *our* plan—but He never fails to provide. Through a grandmother's prayer, a sister-in-law's speed, a toddler's silent understanding, and a car that held out just long enough, we were protected.
In the midst of chaos, there was peace.
And in the middle of our bathroom—there was a miracle.

Chapter 20

Chapter Seven Review

Scripture Verse

John 10:27 (KJV)
"My sheep hear my voice, and I know them, and they follow me."

Reflection

There are moments that don't fit into scientific explanations or human logic. A voice in the early morning, a cry heard across hundreds of miles, a whisper from a loved one in need—these are reminders that we are deeply connected in ways we may never fully understand.

God speaks in the silence. Angels move without fanfare. And love, the purest kind, stretches beyond space and time.

I didn't answer the call with a phone. But I heard it. And I know it was real.

And I believe my father's guardian angel made sure I did.

Chapter 21

Chapter Eight
Review

Scripture Verse

Psalm 91:11 (KJV)

"For he shall give his angels charge over thee, to keep thee in all thy ways."

Reflection

Love does not stop when life does. It continues to echo, to reach, to communicate in mysterious and sacred ways. When we ask for signs, sometimes heaven answers—not with grand gestures, but with quiet certainty.

A phone call in the still of night. A feeling you cannot explain. A peace that arrives exactly when you need it most.

I believe these are not coincidences.

They are connections.

They are promises kept.

They are heaven calling home.

Chapter 22

Chapter Nine Review

Scripture Verse

Romans 8:38–39 (KJV)

"For I am persuaded, that neither death, nor life, nor angels, nor prin-cipalities, nor powers, nor things present, nor things to come... shall be able to separate us from the love of God, which is in Christ Jesus our Lord."

Reflection

There are moments in life when heaven brushes against earth—when love refuses to be silenced by distance or even by death. In that quiet hospital room, with machines humming and time standing still, a father's love found its voice.

Whether it was God's hand, a guardian angel, or something we can't name, one thing is certain: the bond of love is stronger than anything this world can sever.

And sometimes... it sings.

Chapter 23

Chapter Ten Review

Scripture Verse

Psalm 121:7–8 (KJV)

"The Lord shall preserve thee from all evil: he shall preserve thy soul. The Lord shall preserve thy going out and thy coming in from this time forth, and even for evermore."

Reflection

There are moments in life when you see the line between disaster and survival—when you know just how close you came. For us, that line was held together by the grace of God and the unseen hands of a guardian angel.

If you're a parent, you know this truth in your bones: we cannot protect our children from everything. But we can pray. We can trust. We can believe that even when we fail to see, someone else is watching.

And sometimes, that someone catches your child when the world lets them fall.

Chapter 24

Chapter Eleven Review

Scripture Verse

Psalm 91:11-12 (KJV)

"For he shall give his angels charge over thee, to keep thee in all thy ways.
They shall bear thee up in their hands, lest thou dash thy foot against a stone."

Reflection
So yes, once again, we were given:
A happy ending.
A chance to avoid a painful surgery.
A reminder that guardian angels don't always wear wings—they might just hover silently in the background, nudging a child to stay still, to trust their body, to wait.
And as a mother, I'll take **all the help I can get**.
Because raising boys is hard enough.
But raising boys under the watchful care of something divine?

Now that's a blessing I'll never stop being grateful for.

Chapter 25

Chapter Twelve Review

Scripture Verse

1 Thessalonians 4:13-14 (KJV)

"But I would not have you to be ignorant, brethren, concerning them which are asleep, that ye sorrow not, even as others which have no hope.
For if we believe that Jesus died and rose again, even so them also which sleep in Jesus will God bring with him."

Reflection

When someone we love passes suddenly, we often replay everything we said—and didn't say. The regret, the unanswered questions, the aching silence can feel unbearable.

But sometimes, God allows one last moment. A flicker of connection. A divine appointment not marked by clocks or phone records but by **spirit and love**.

That moment with Mike wasn't something I imagined. It was something I received.

And it carried me through the heartbreak.

The bond of love doesn't end when life does. It changes shape. It softens and deepens and continues to speak—sometimes in dreams, sometimes in silence, sometimes through a call that never came, but still somehow arrived.

Chapter 26

Angel Verses from the Bible

All throughout Scripture, God shows us that we are never alone. Though we cannot always see them, His angels are present — messengers of hope, protectors in danger, and quiet companions on the journey of faith. The Bible describes angels surrounding those who love and trust the Lord, guiding paths, strengthening hearts, and even fighting unseen battles on our behalf.

These verses remind us of a comforting truth: God's care for His children is tender and active. He commands His angels concerning us, sends them ahead to prepare the way, and surrounds us with their presence when we feel vulnerable or afraid. As you read each passage, pause to let its promise sink in. The prayers will help you speak back to God, thanking Him for His protection and asking for deeper trust in His unseen work.

May these words draw you closer to the Father who watches over you and give you courage to walk in peace, knowing heaven is nearer than you think.

Chapter 27

Psalm 91:11

"For he shall give his angels charge over thee, to keep thee in all thy ways."

Meaning: God appoints His angels to protect and guide us throughout our lives. This verse is a powerful reminder that divine protection is always surrounding us, even when we don't see it.

Prayer: Heavenly Father, thank You for appointing Your angels to watch over me. Help me to trust in Your protection and walk boldly, knowing I am never alone. Amen.

Chapter 28

Hebrews 1:14

"Are they not all ministering spirits, sent forth to minister for them who shall be heirs of salvation?"

Meaning: Angels are God's servants, assigned to help and serve those who believe in Him. They are heavenly messengers acting on behalf of God's children.

Prayer: Lord, thank You for sending Your angels to serve and guide me. May I always be mindful of their presence and walk in the assurance of Your care. Amen.

Chapter 29

Matthew 18:10

"Take heed that ye despise not one of these little ones; for I say unto you, That in heaven their angels do always behold the face of my Father which is in heaven."

Meaning: Children are especially dear to God, and each one is guarded by an angel who has direct access to the Father. This shows the great value and protection God places on the vulnerable.

Prayer: Father, thank You for loving and protecting children. Help me to treat them with kindness and respect, knowing they are precious in Your sight. Amen.

Chapter 30

Acts 12:7

"And, behold, the angel of the Lord came upon him, and a light shined in the prison: and he smote Peter on the side, and raised him up, saying, Arise up quickly. And his chains fell off from his hands."

Meaning: Angels can bring deliverance in times of distress. Just as Peter was freed from prison, we too can trust that God can send help at just the right time.

Prayer: Lord, when I feel trapped or burdened, remind me of Your power to deliver. Thank You for sending angels to break my chains and set me free. Amen

Chapter 31

Exodus 23:20

"Behold, I send an Angel before thee, to keep thee in the way, and to bring thee into the place which I have prepared."

Meaning: God promises His guidance and protection through His angels as we journey through life.

Prayer: Gracious God, guide me through the paths You've prepared, and let Your angels lead me safely to Your will. Amen.

Chapter 32

Daniel 6:22

"My God hath sent his angel, and hath shut the lions' mouths, that they have not hurt me."

Meaning: God's angels intervene in miraculous ways to protect His faithful servants from danger.

Prayer:
Almighty God, I trust in Your power to deliver me from harm. Thank You for Your angels, who are my defenders. Amen.

Chapter 33

Genesis 32:1

"And Jacob went on his way, and the angels of God met him."

Meaning: Angels are sent to meet us on our journey, offering reassurance of God's presence.

Prayer:
Lord, as I walk through life's challenges, may I meet the angels You send to remind me of Your constant care. Amen.

Chapter 34

Acts 12:7

"And, behold, the angel of the Lord came upon him, and a light shined in the prison: and he smote Peter on the side, and raised him up, saying, Arise up quickly. And his chains fell off from his hands."

Meaning: Angels are sent to bring deliverance and freedom to God's people in times of distress.

Prayer:
Merciful Father, thank You for the angels who deliver me from spiritual and physical bondage. May I rise with faith to follow Your light. Amen.

Chapter 35

2 Kings 6:17

"And Elisha prayed, and said, Lord, I pray thee, open his eyes, that he may see. And the Lord opened the eyes of the young man; and he saw: and, behold, the mountain was full of horses and chariots of fire round about Elisha."

Meaning: God's angels surround and protect us, even when we cannot see them.

Prayer:
Lord, open my eyes to see Your heavenly protection around me. Help me to trust in Your power, even when I cannot see it. Amen.

Chapter 36

Revelation 5:11

"And I beheld, and I heard the voice of many angels round about the throne and the beasts and the elders: and the number of them was ten thousand times ten thousand, and thousands of thousands."

Meaning: Heaven is filled with angels who worship God continually. Their presence reminds us of the majesty and glory of the Lord, and the unending praise He is worthy of.

Prayer: Holy God, thank You for the heavenly host that surrounds Your throne in worship. Help me to join in that praise, living a life that honors You each day. Amen.

Chapter 37

Exercise

Take the following blank pages to jot down times when you believe angels interceded in your life.

How did this make you feel?

Have you shared this experience with others?

About The Author

Karen Kazimer Shockley is a passionate author who has touched the hearts of readers with her inspiring books centered on celebrating holidays, heartfelt romances, and uplifting stories about Christianity. Her works beautifully weave together faith, love, and the joy of special moments, creating stories that resonate with readers of all ages.